This Book Belongs To:

Color Test Page

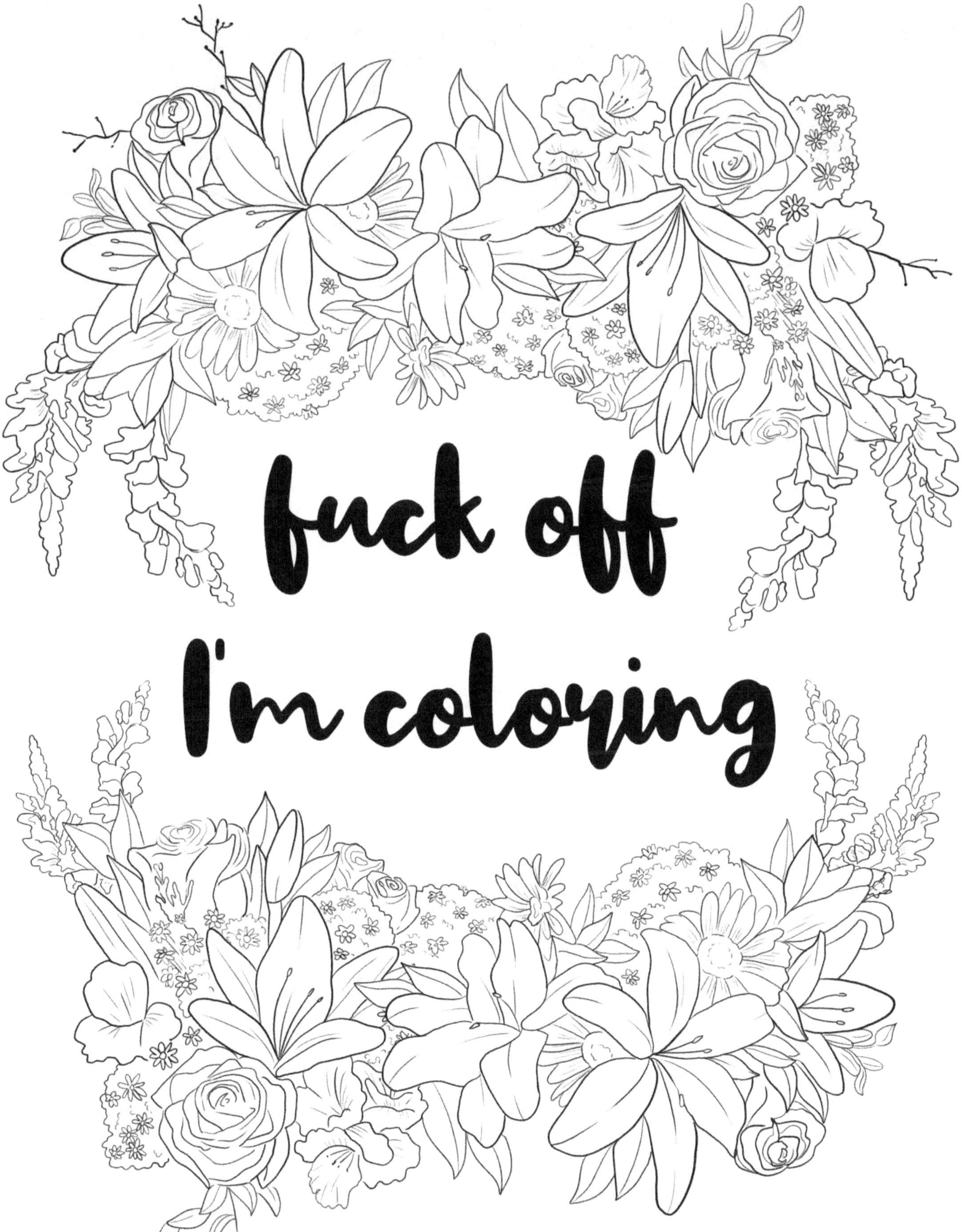
fuck off
I'm coloring

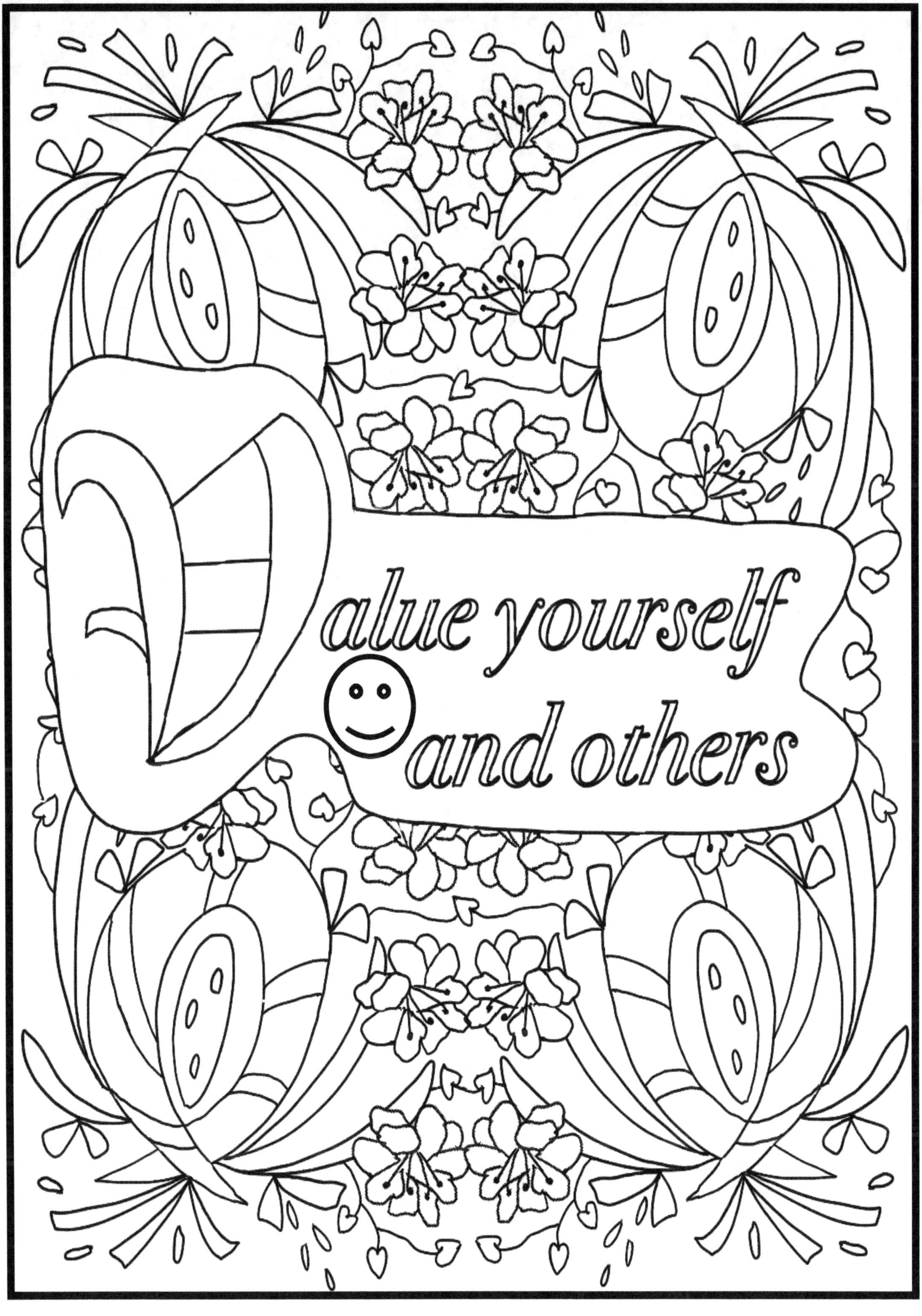
Value yourself
and others

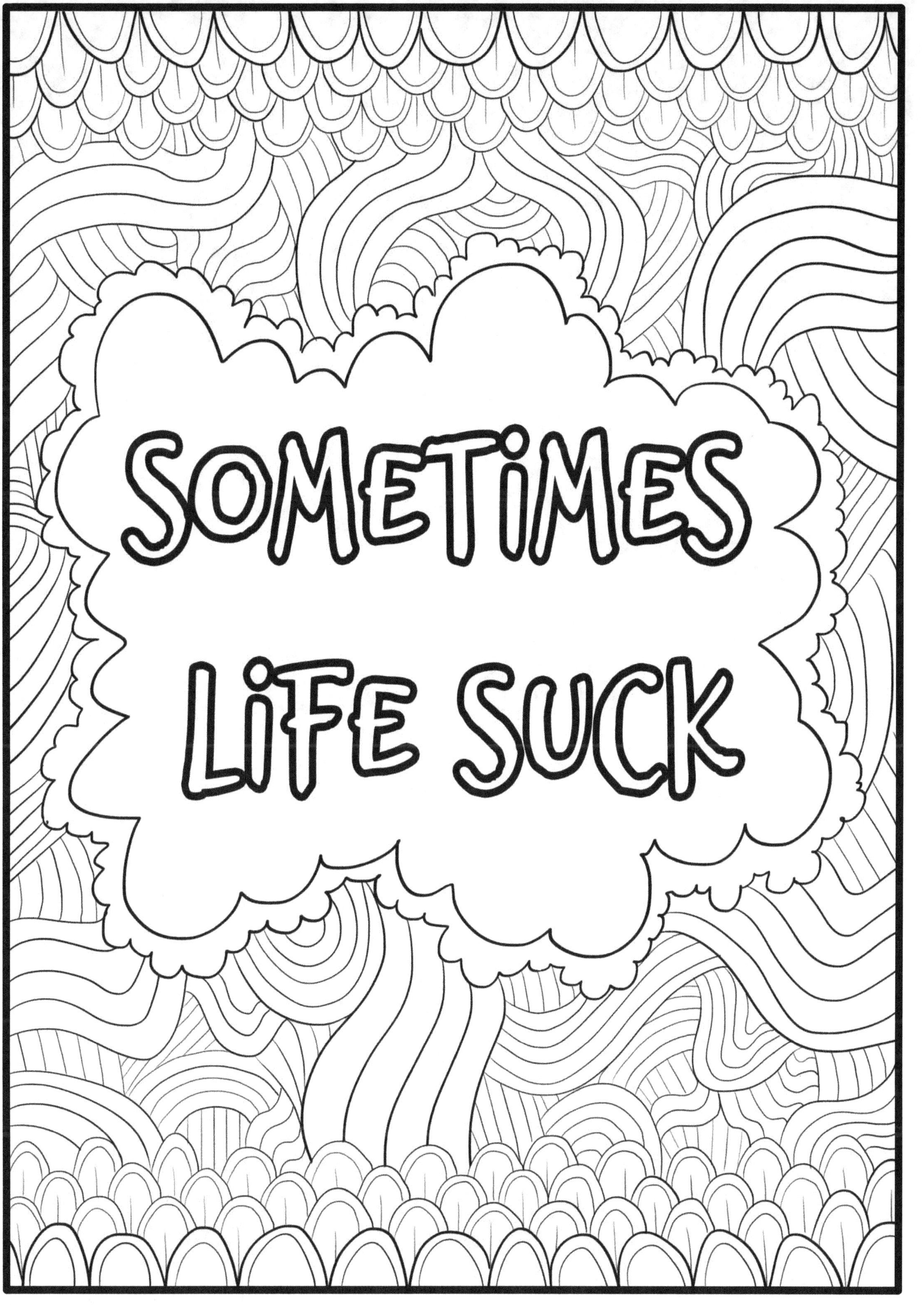
SOMETIMES LIFE SUCK

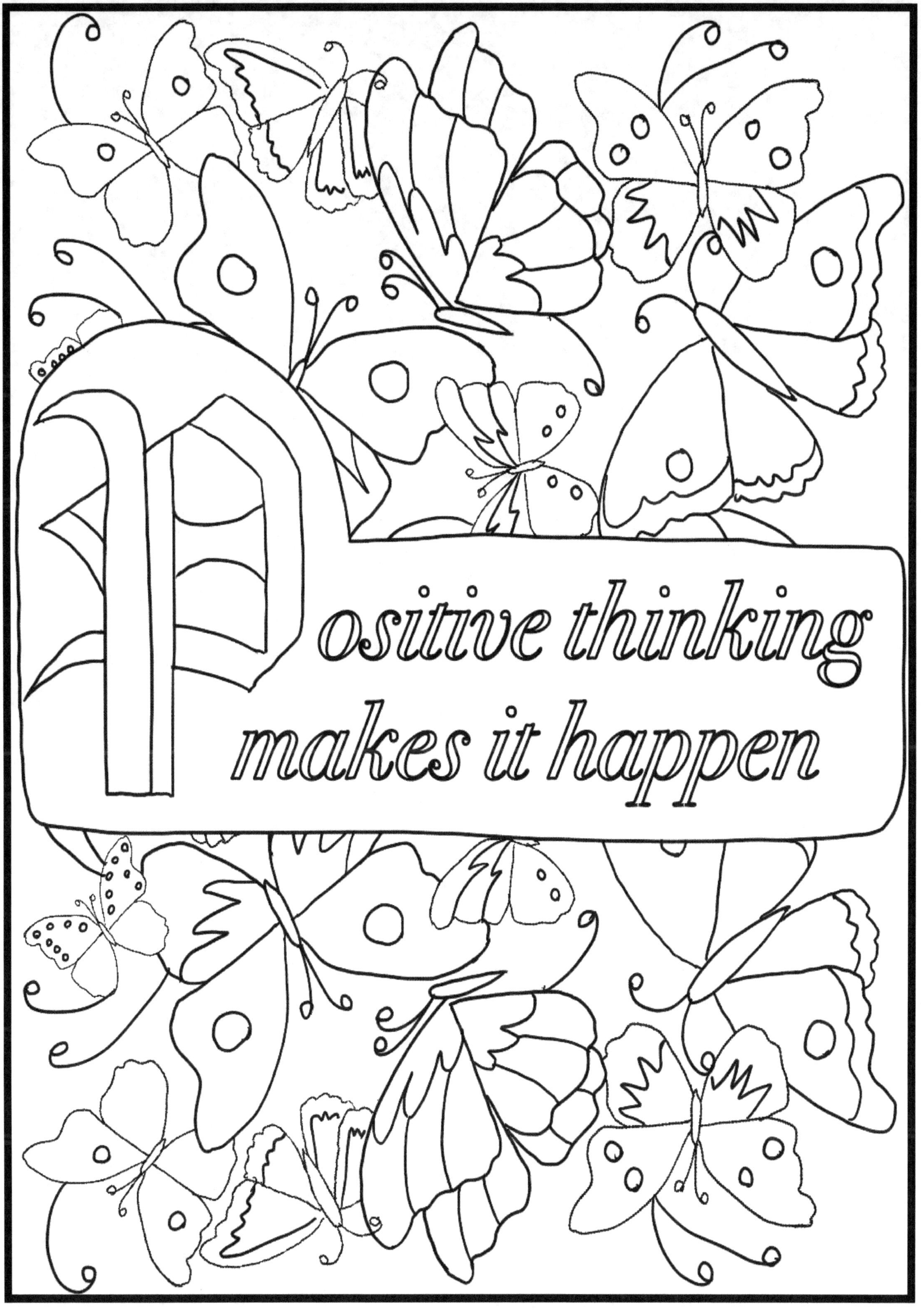
Positive thinking
makes it happen

Adopt the pace of nature: her secret is patience.

- Ralph Waldo Emerson

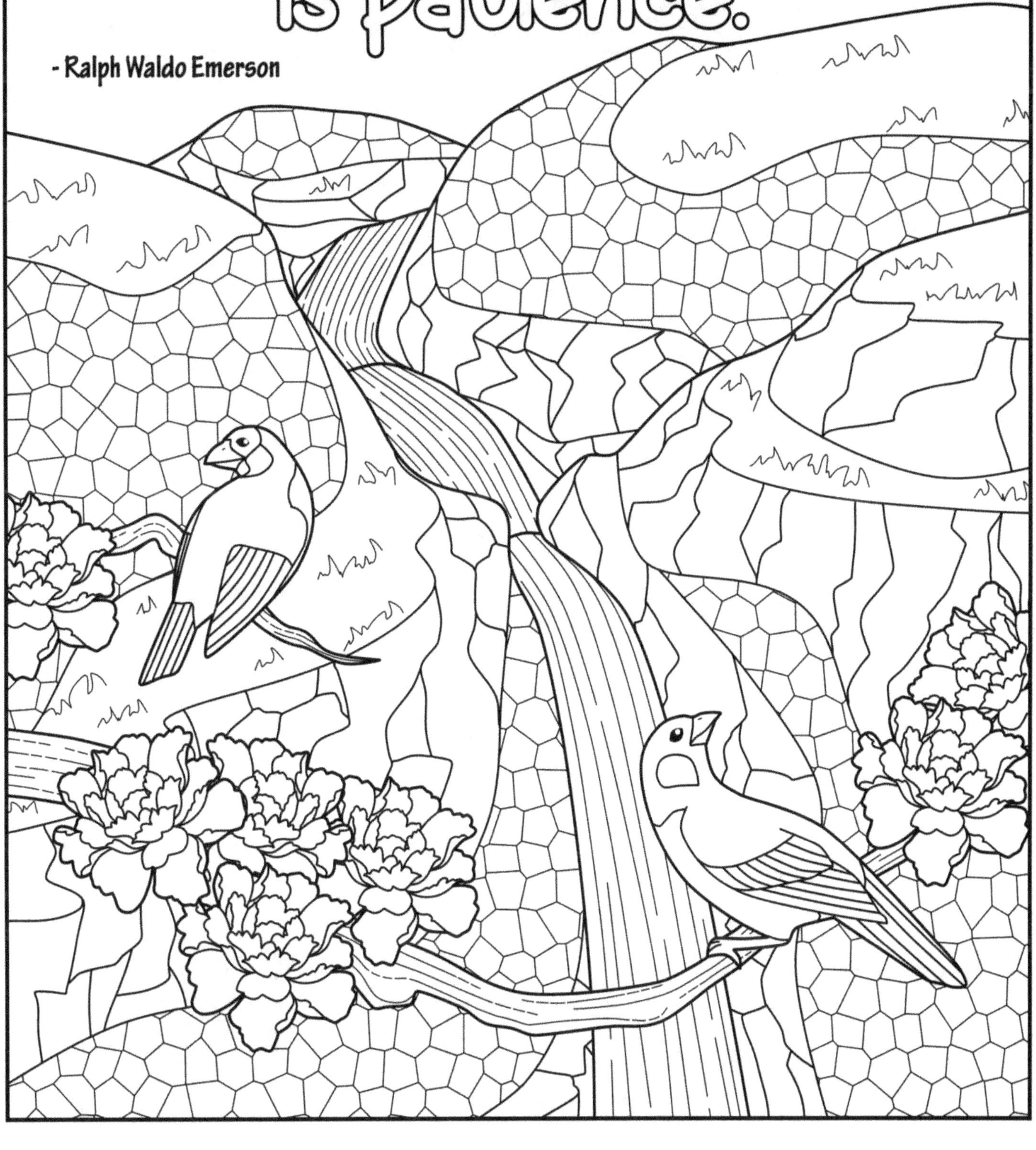

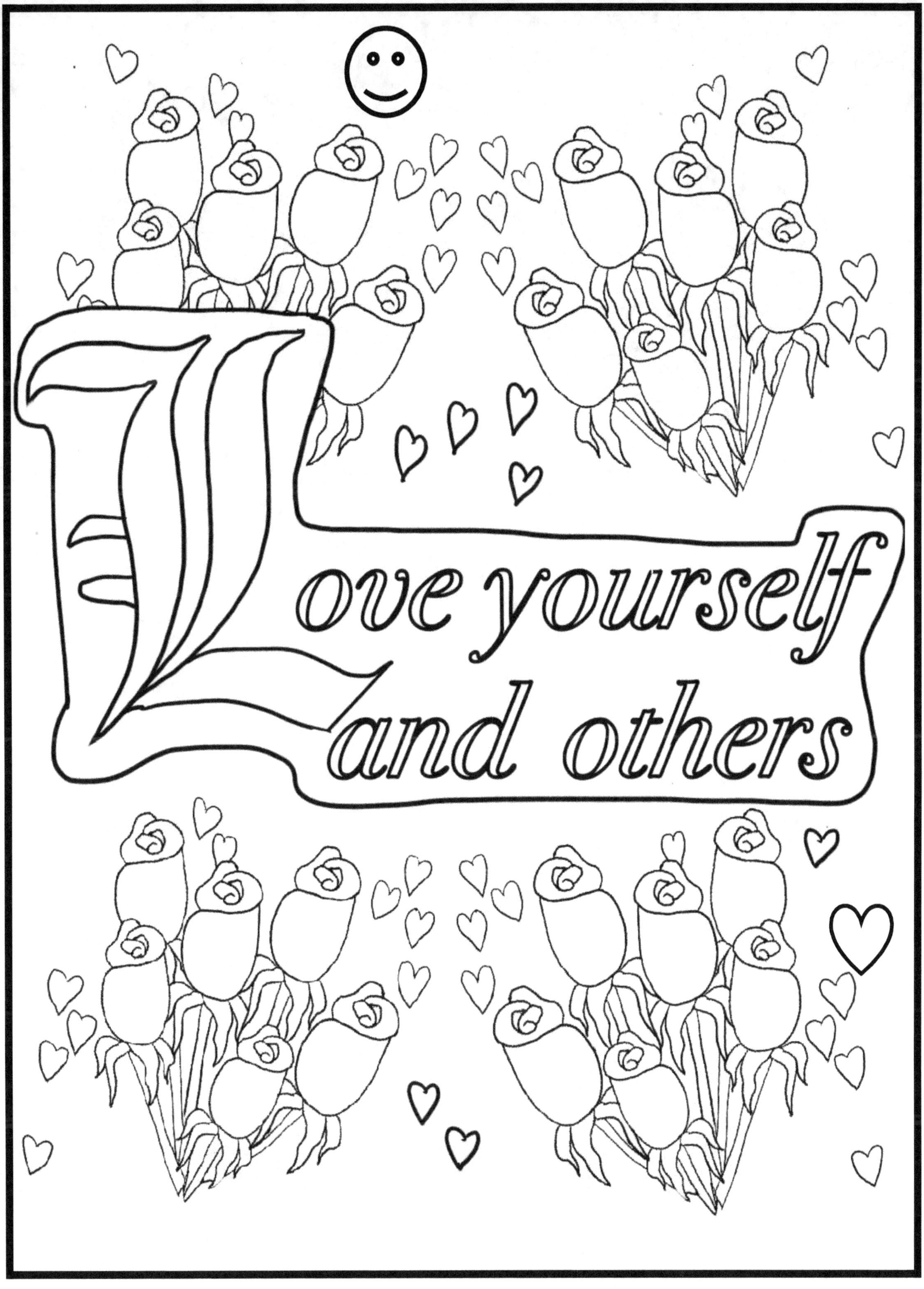
Love yourself
and others

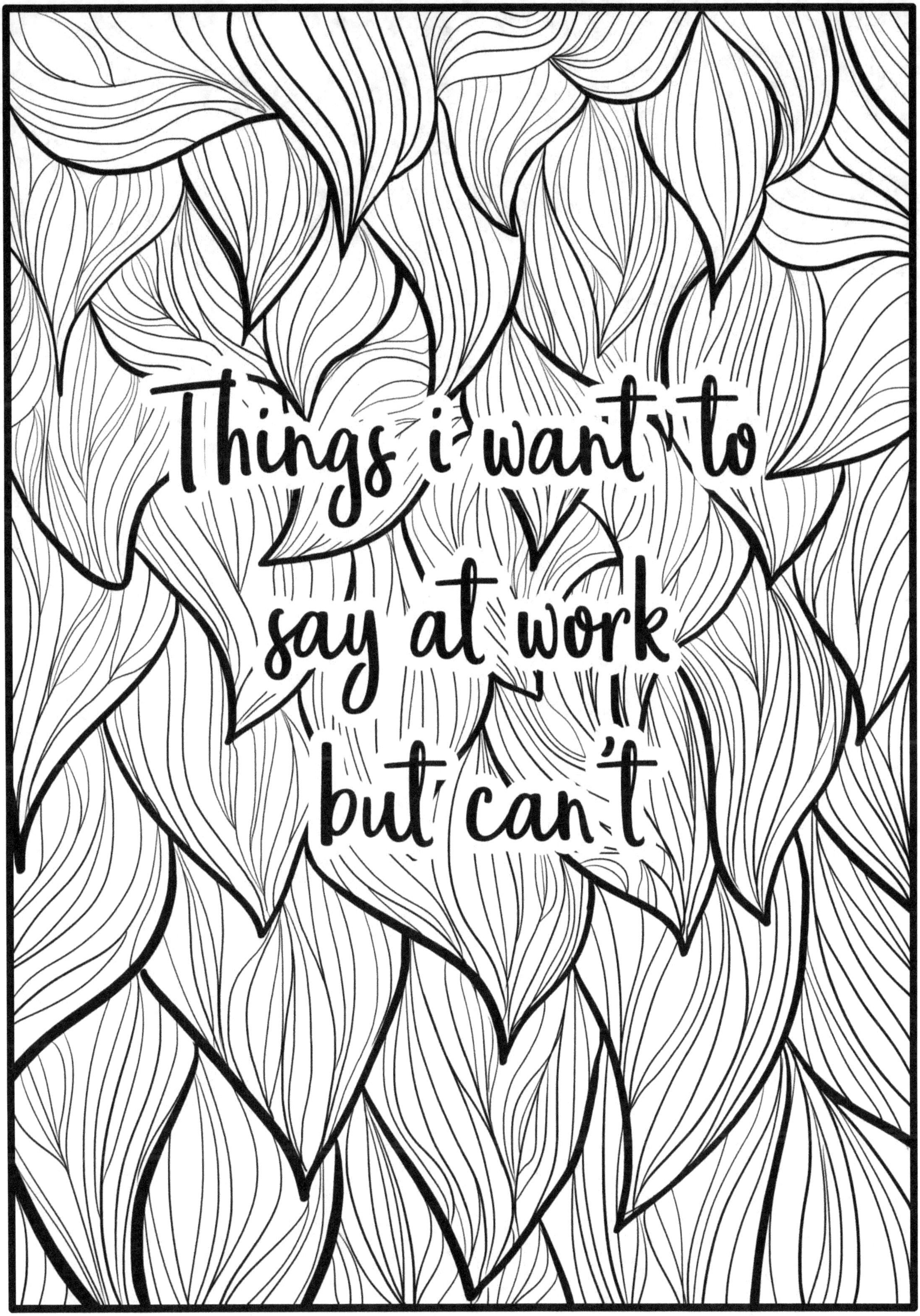
Things i want to
say at work
but can't

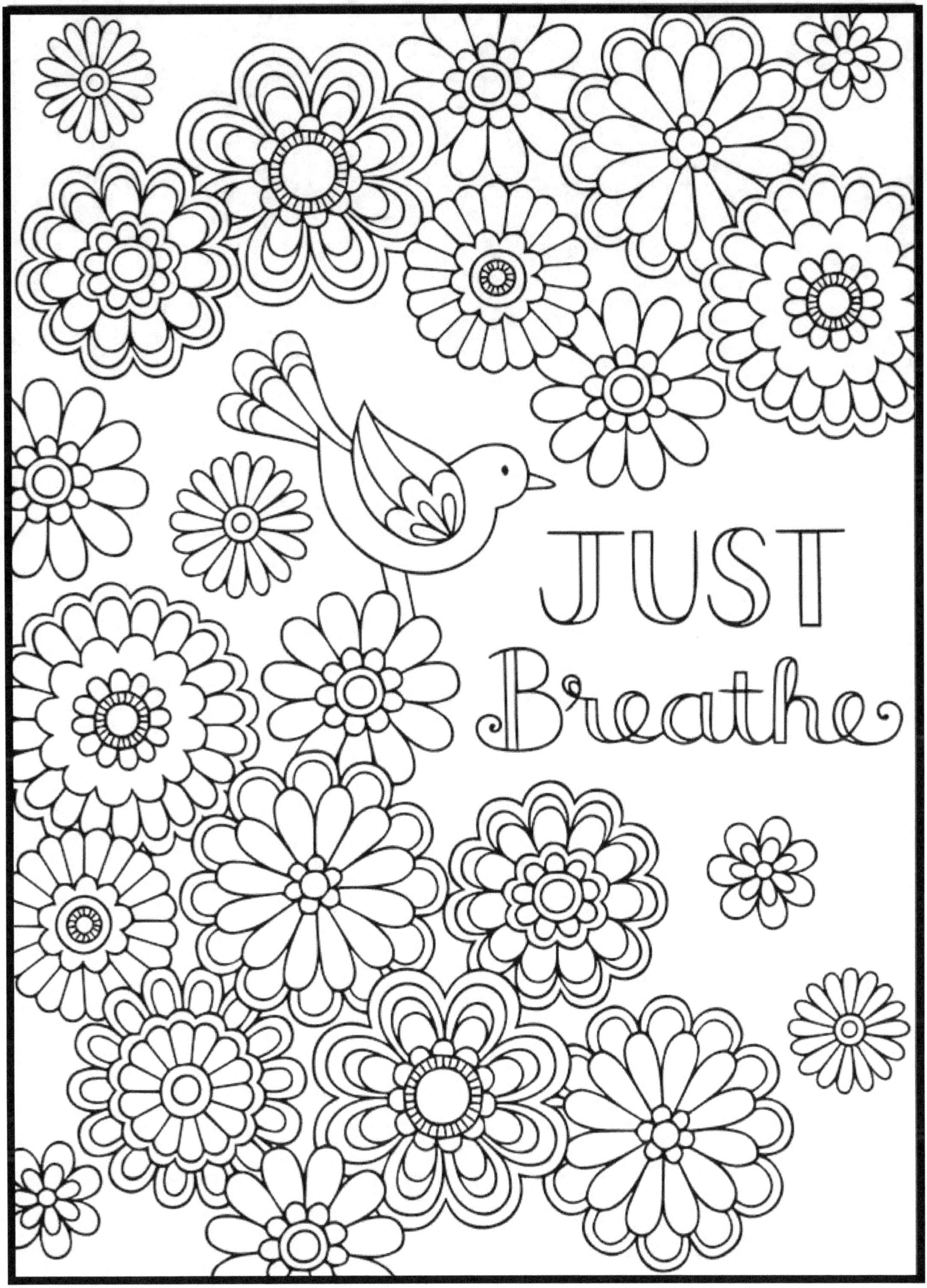
JUST
Breathe

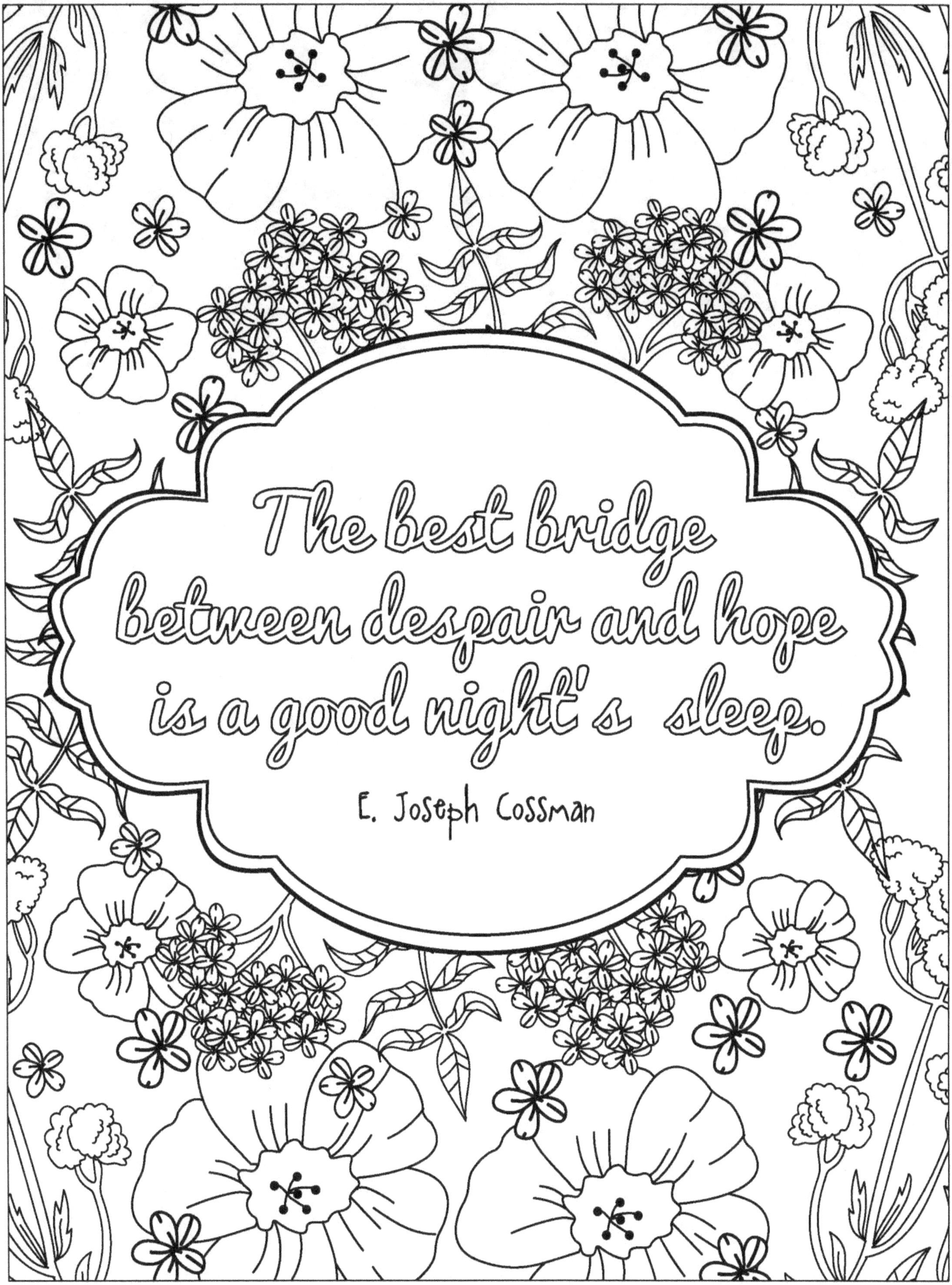
The best bridge
between despair and hope
is a good night's sleep.
E. Joseph Cossman

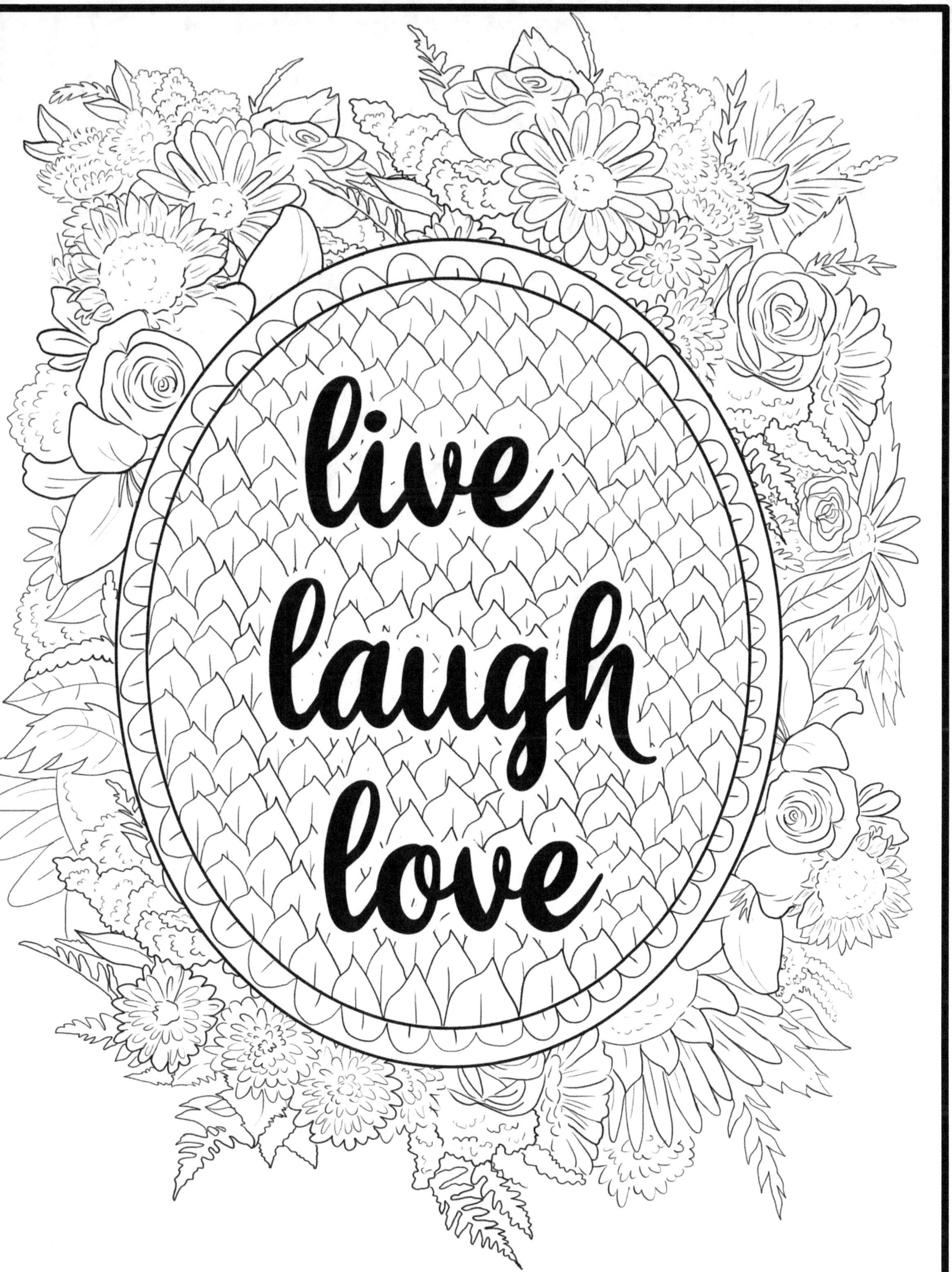
live
laugh
love

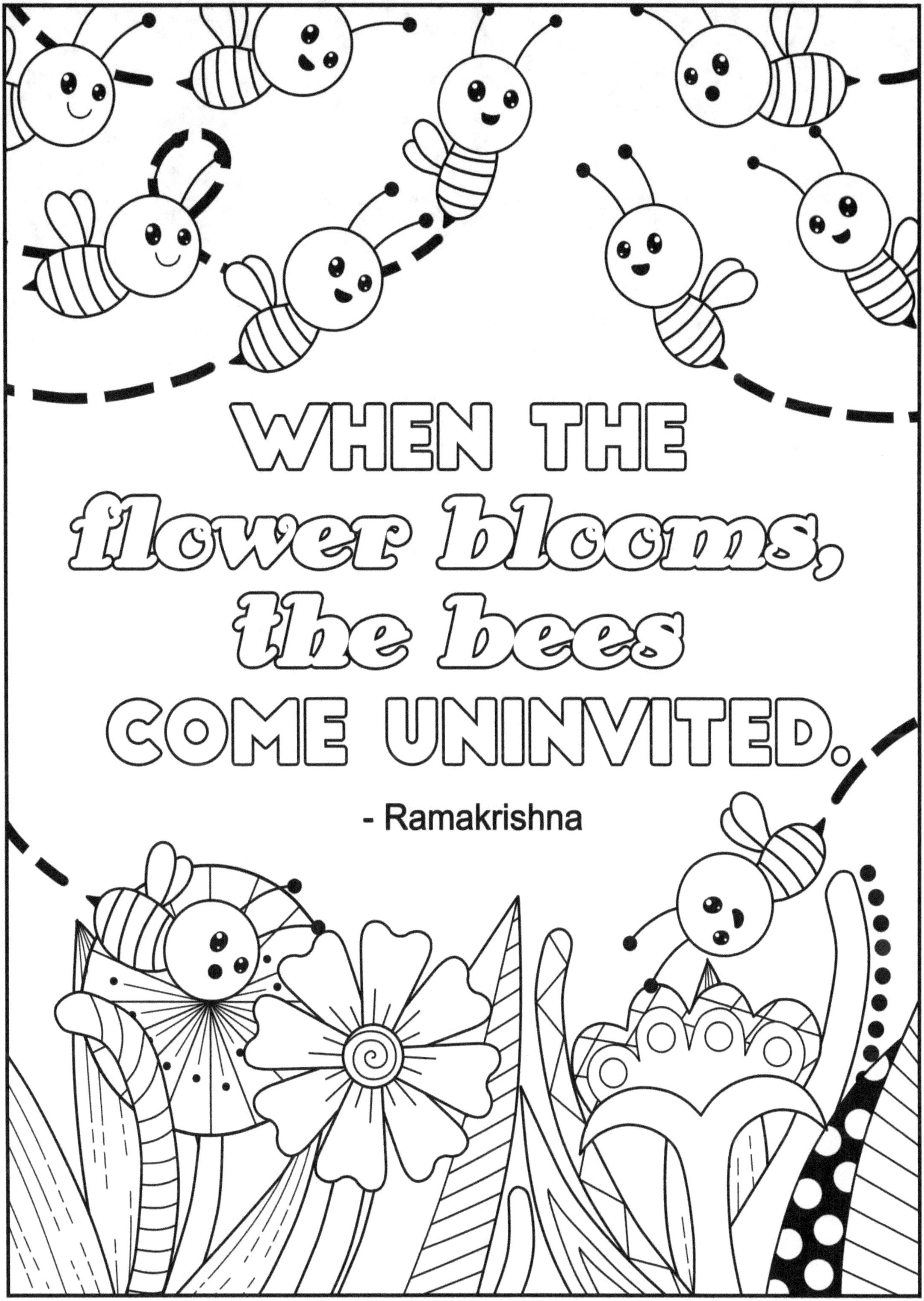
WHEN THE
flower blooms,
the bees
COME UNINVITED.
- Ramakrishna

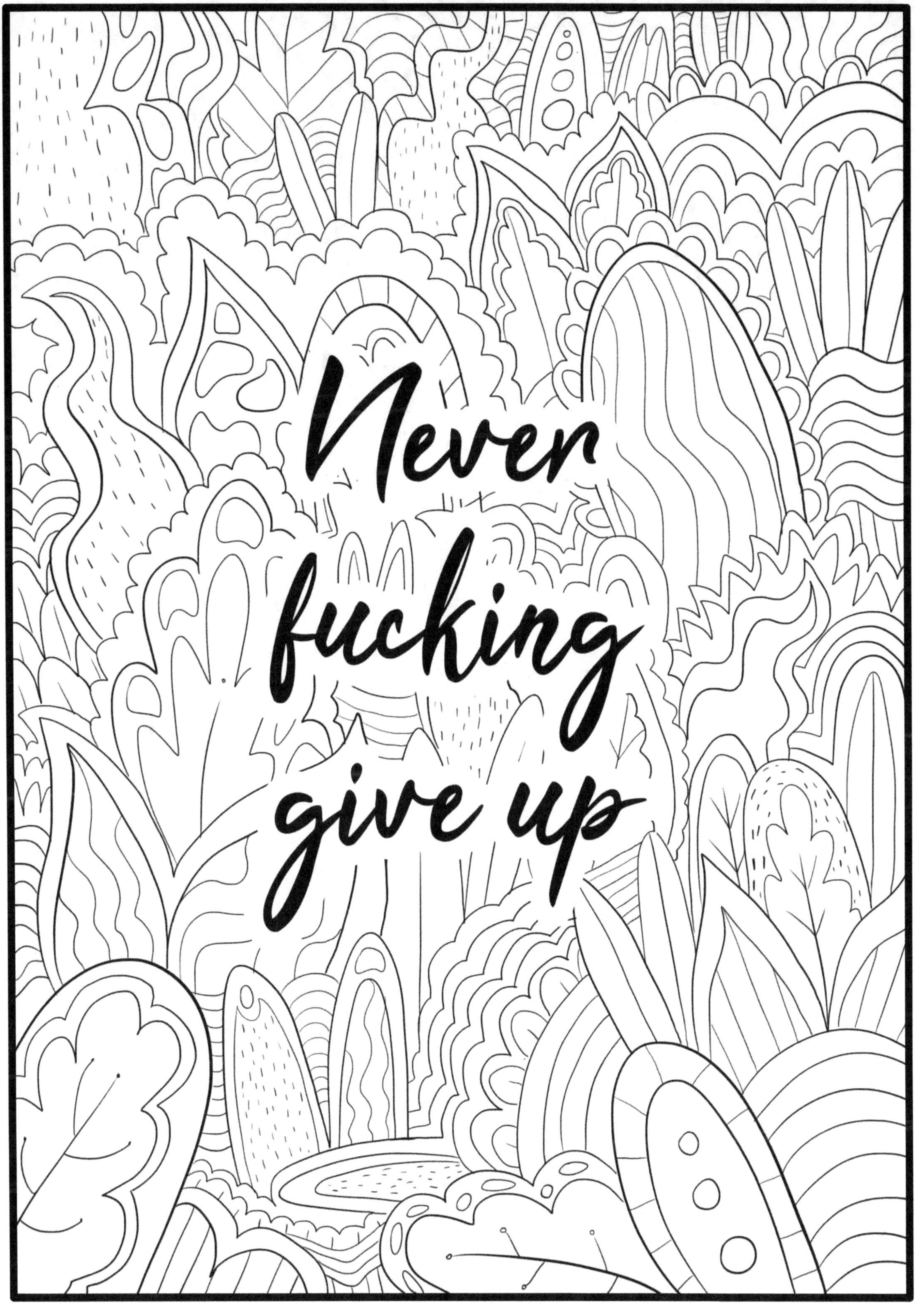
Never
fucking
give up

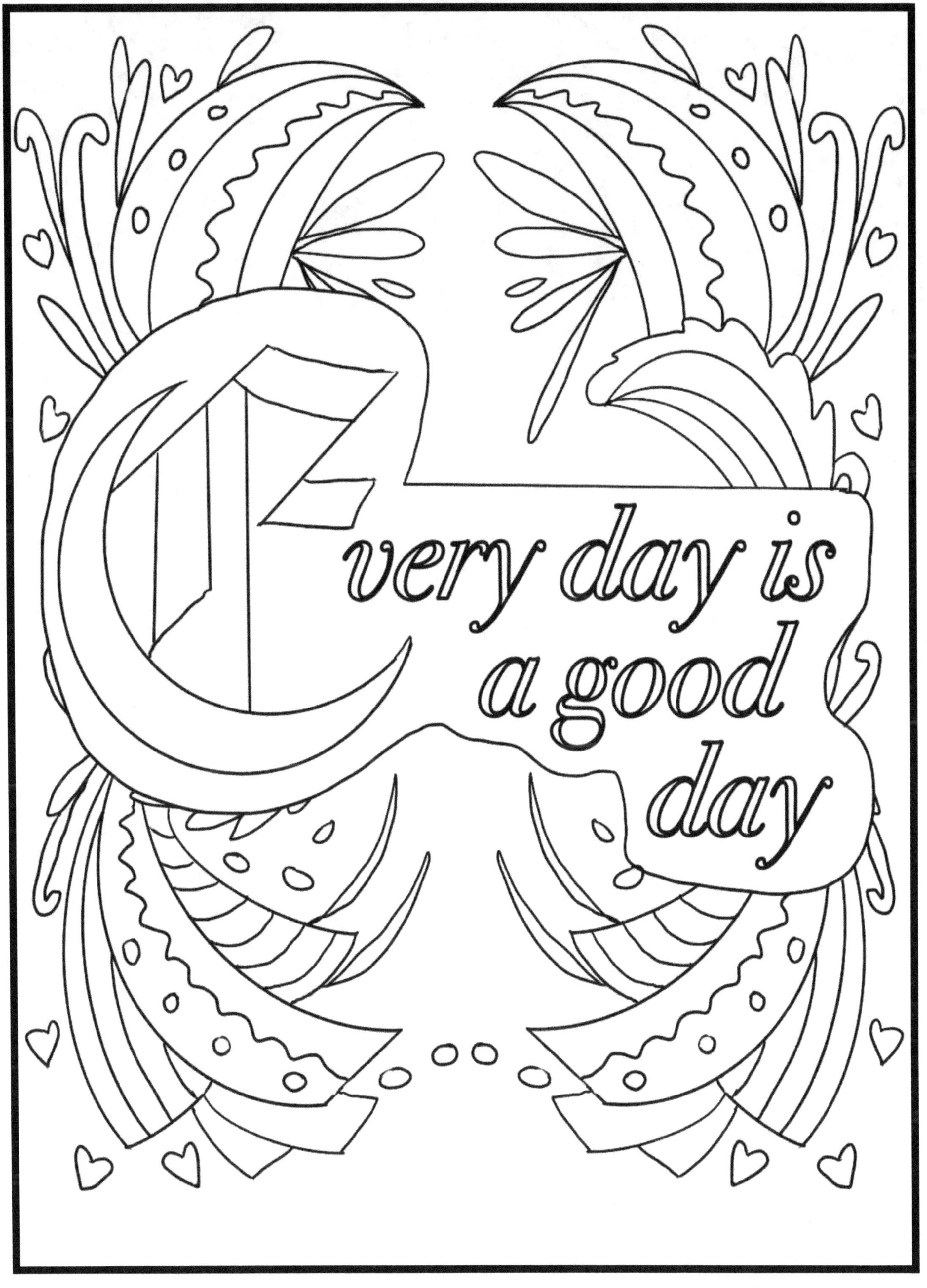
Every day is
a good
day

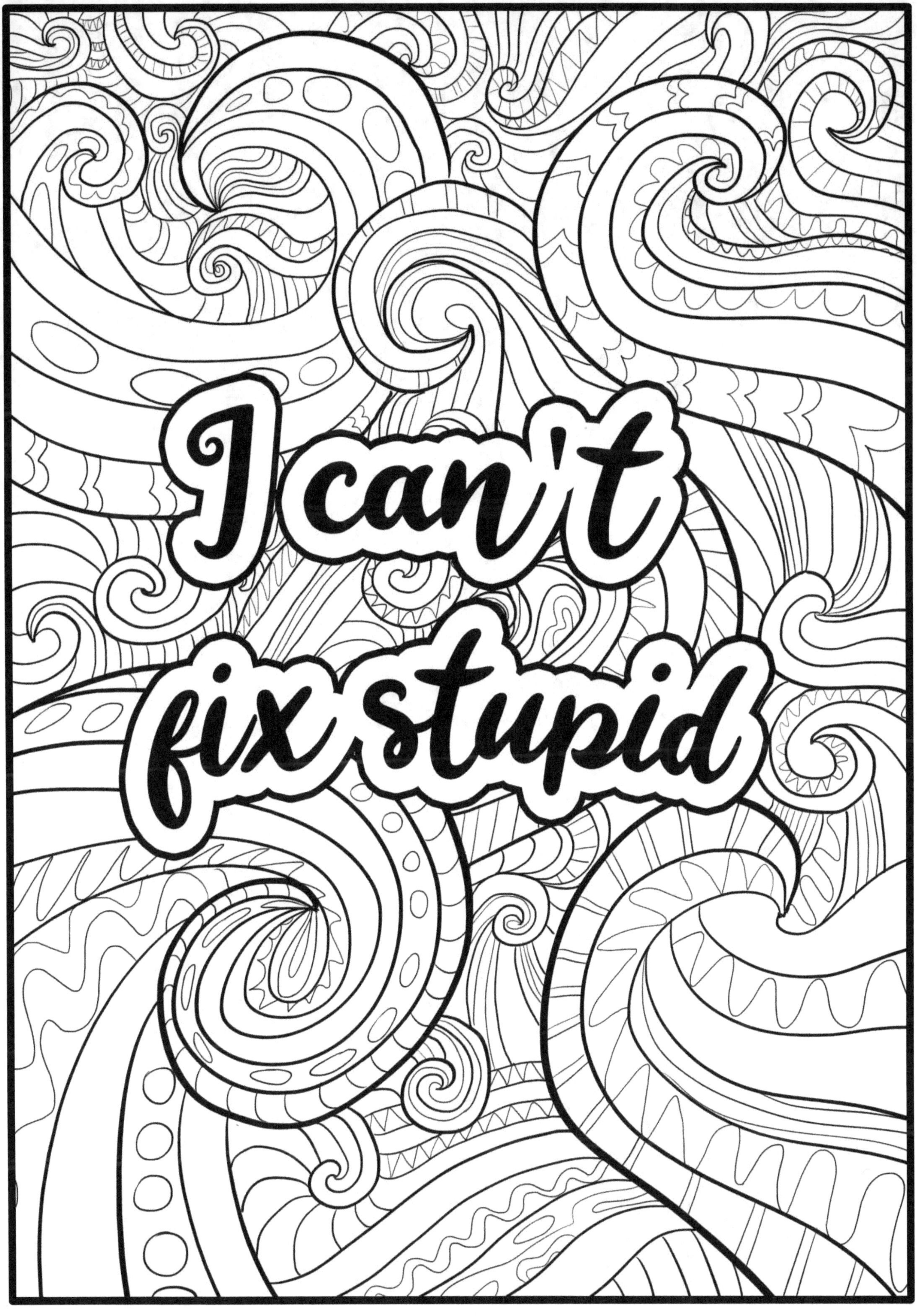
I can't
fix stupid

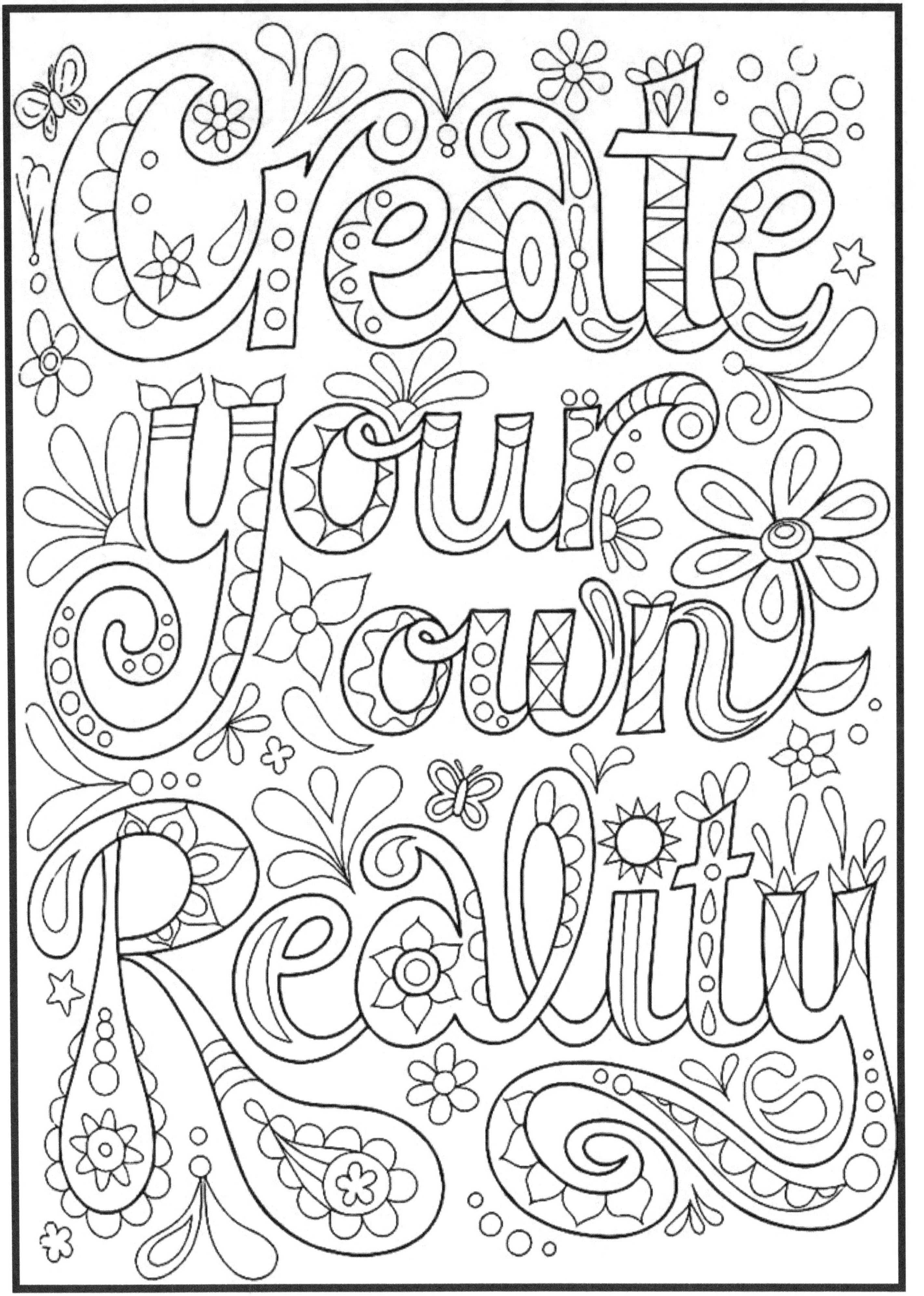
Create your own Reality

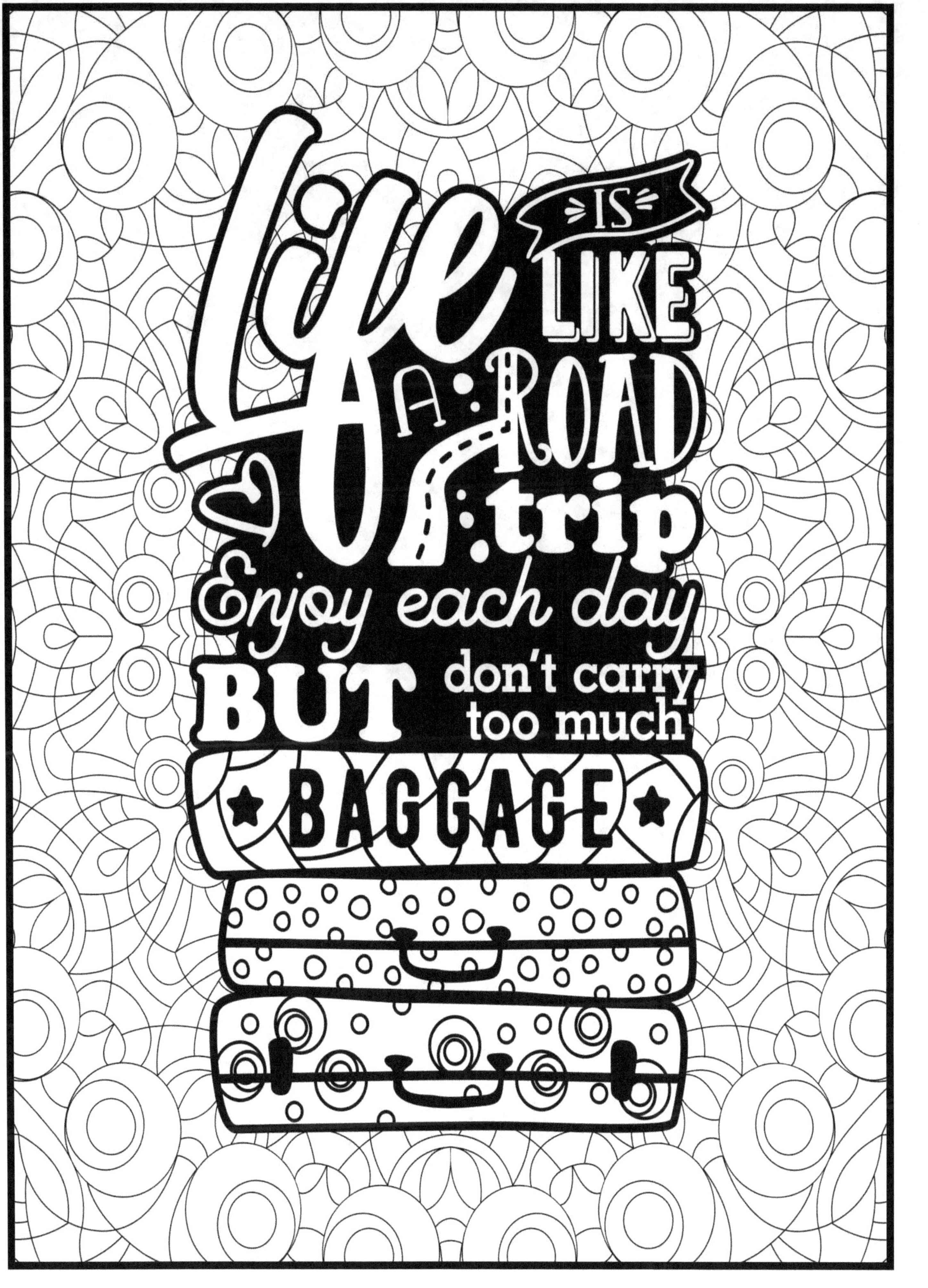
Life
IS
LIKE
A ROAD
trip
Enjoy each day
BUT
don't carry
too much
BAGGAGE

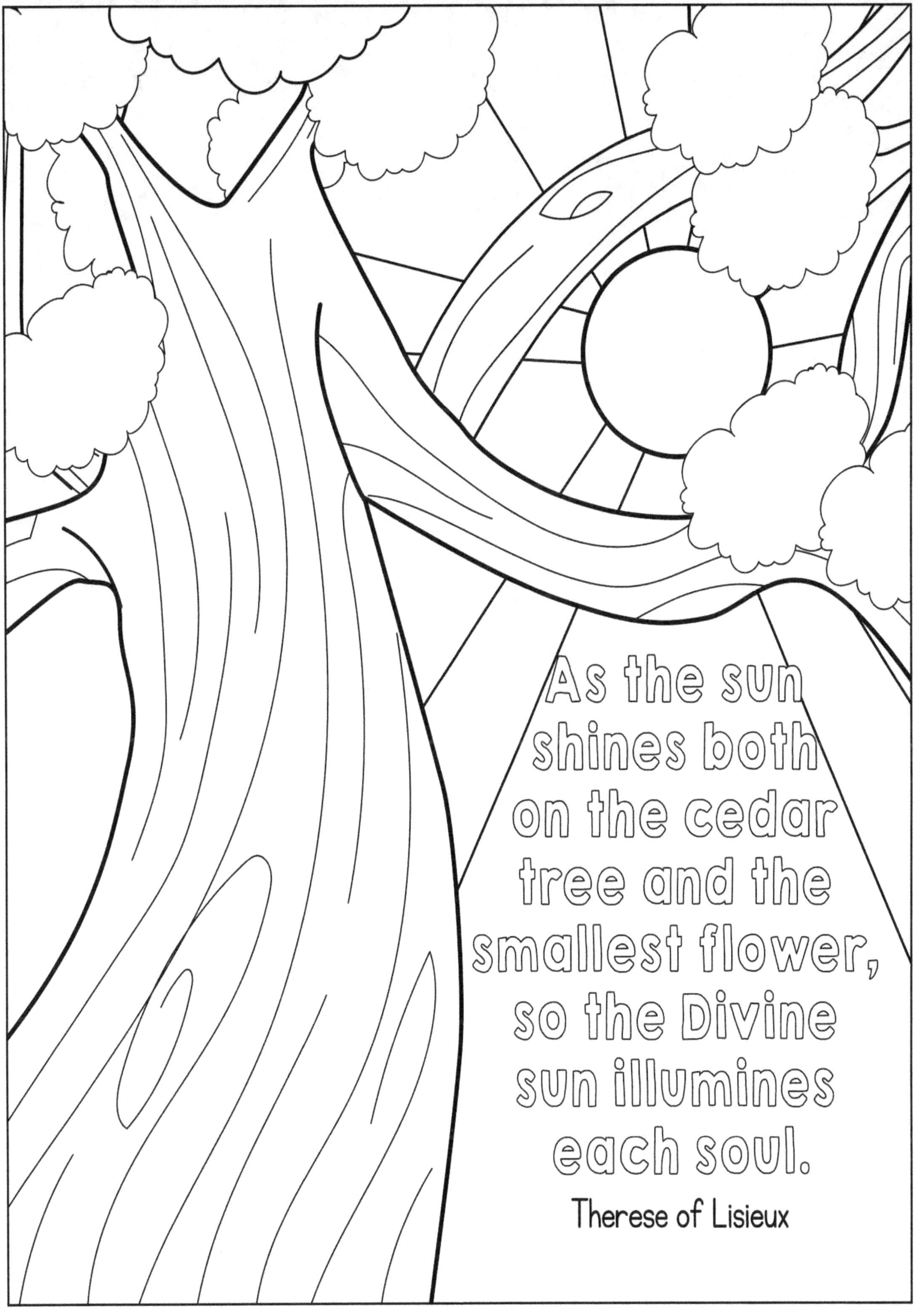
As the sun shines both on the cedar tree and the smallest flower, so the Divine sun illumines each soul.
Therese of Lisieux

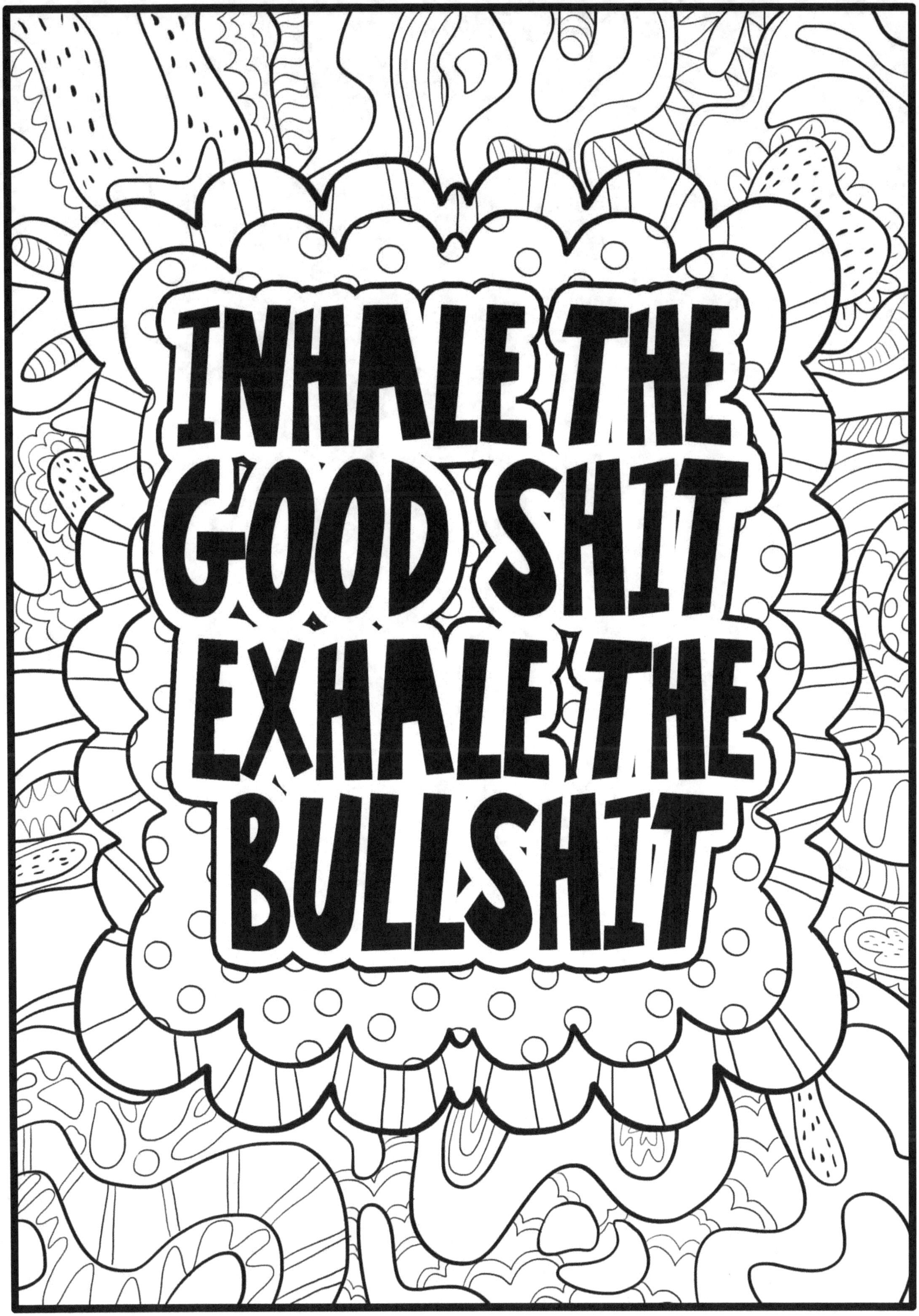
INHALE THE
GOOD SHIT
EXHALE THE
BULLSHIT

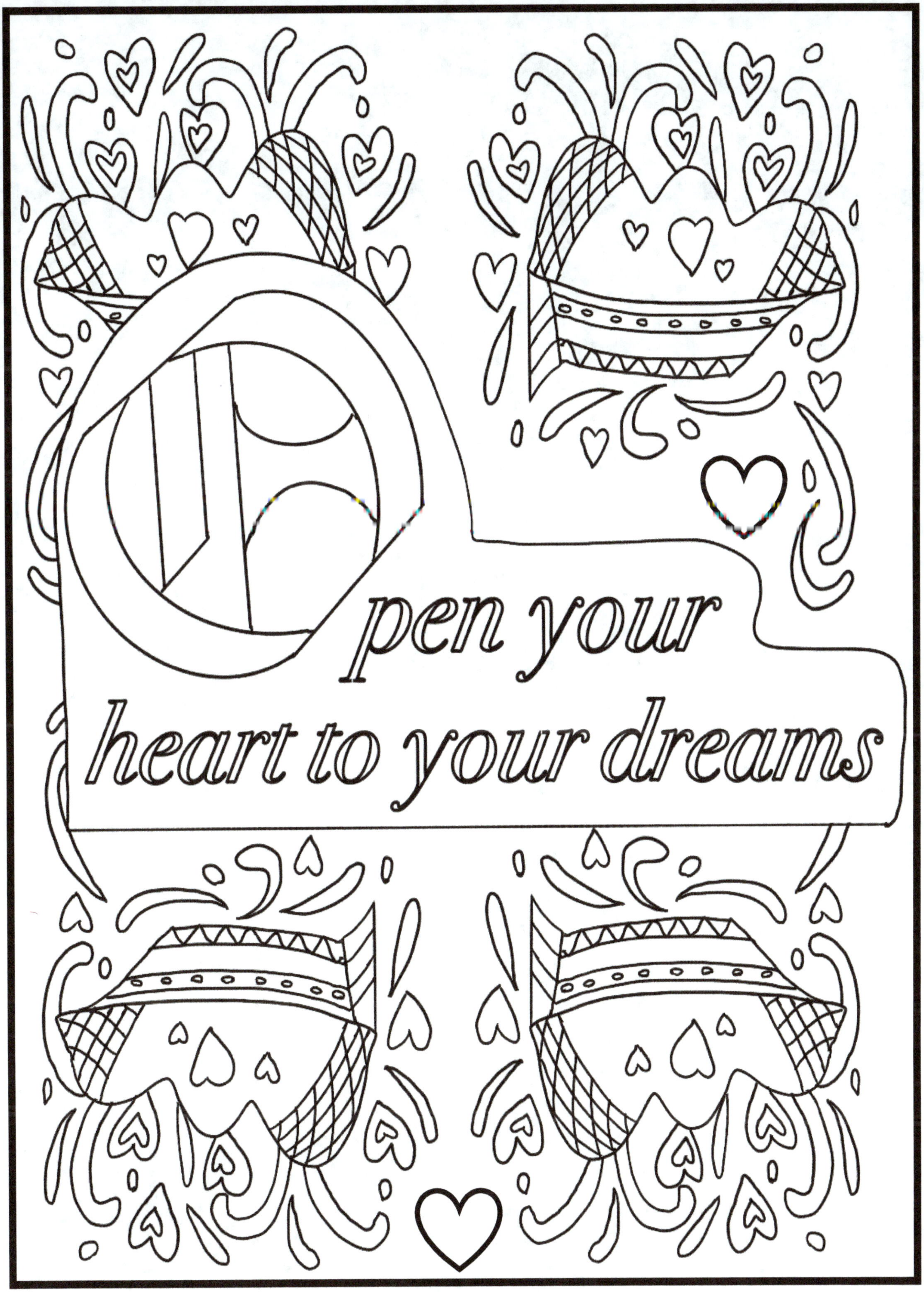
Open your
heart to your dreams

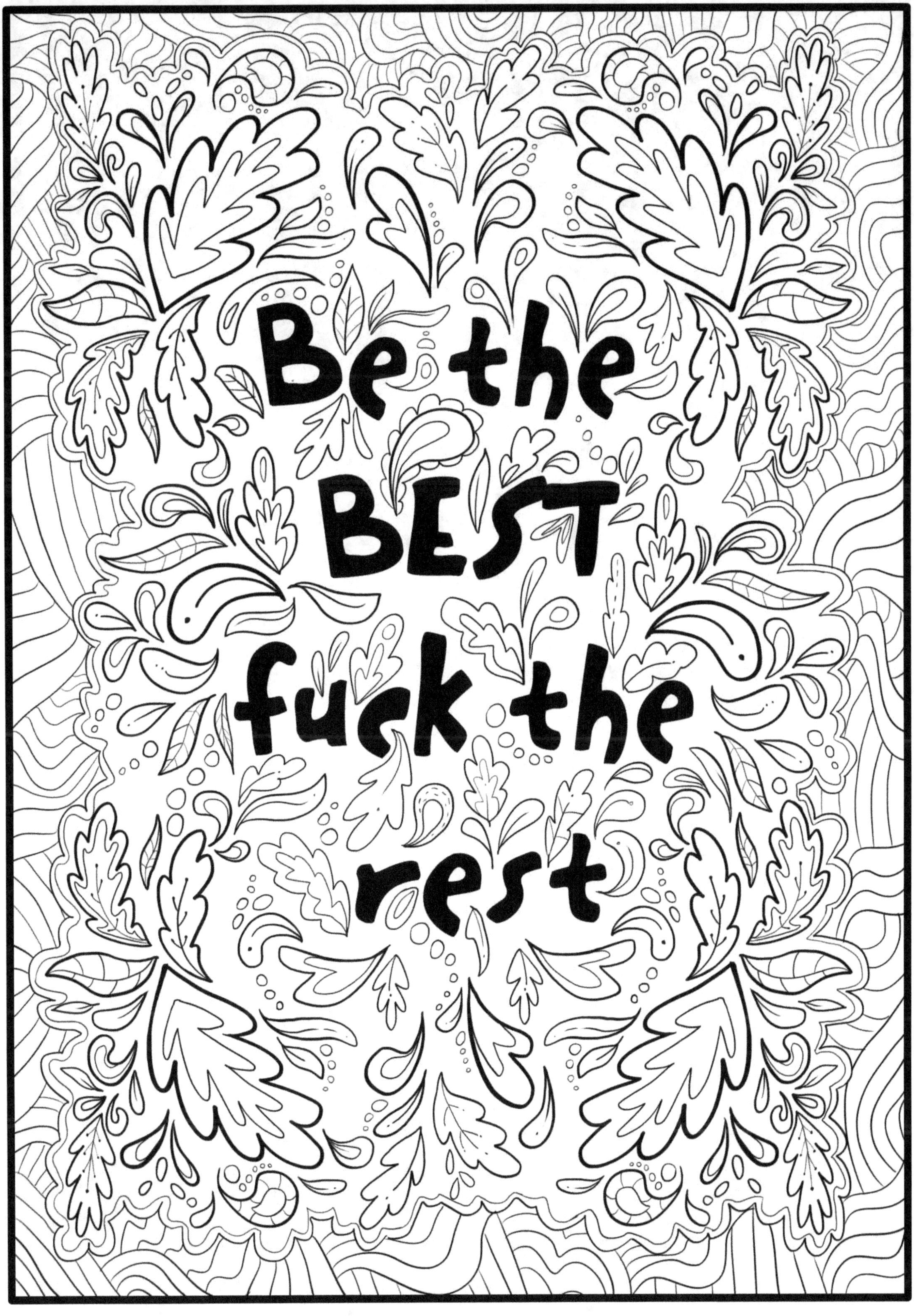
Be the
BEST
fuck the
rest

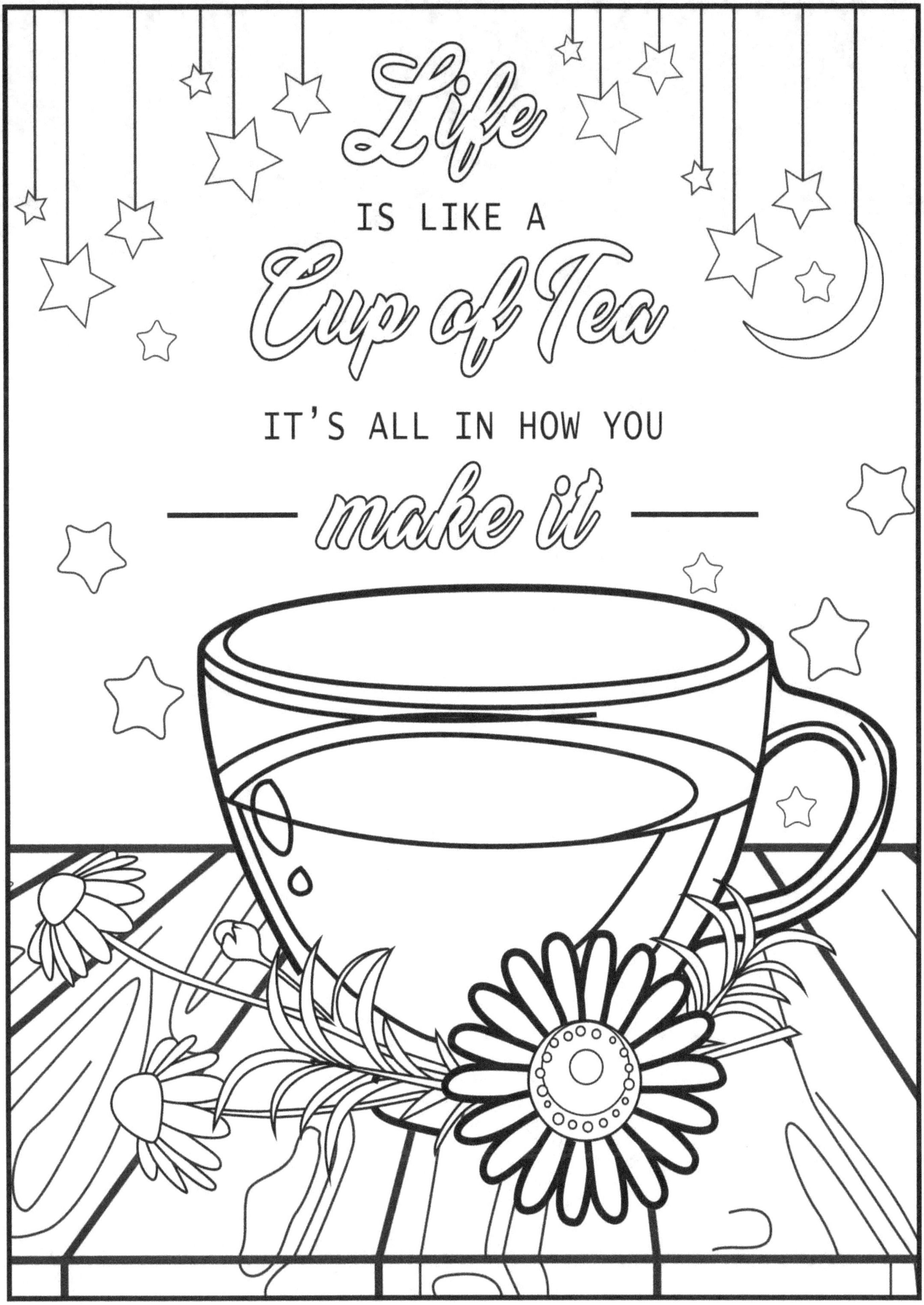
Life
IS LIKE A
Cup of Tea
IT'S ALL IN HOW YOU
make it

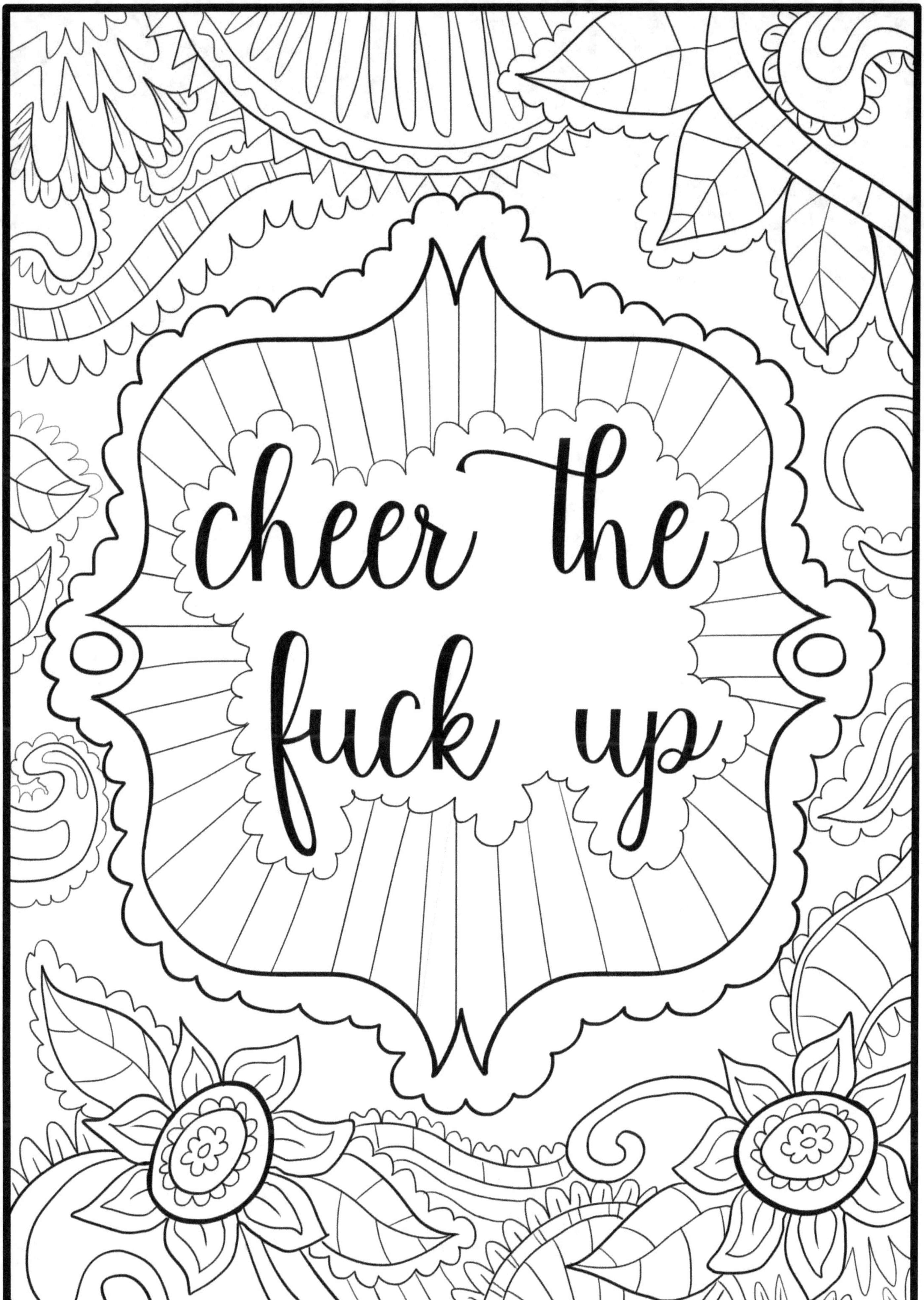
cheer the
fuck up

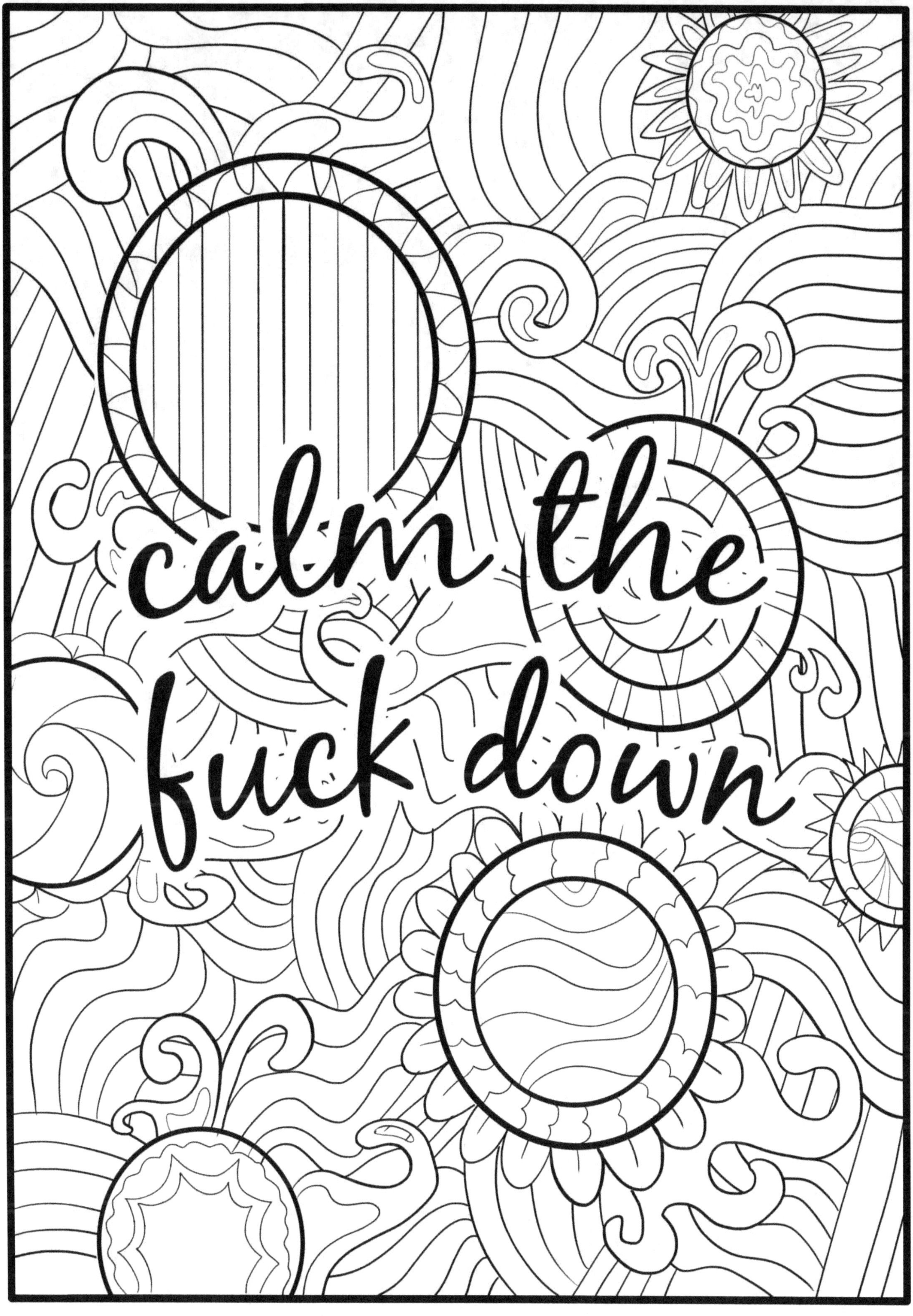
calm the
fuck down

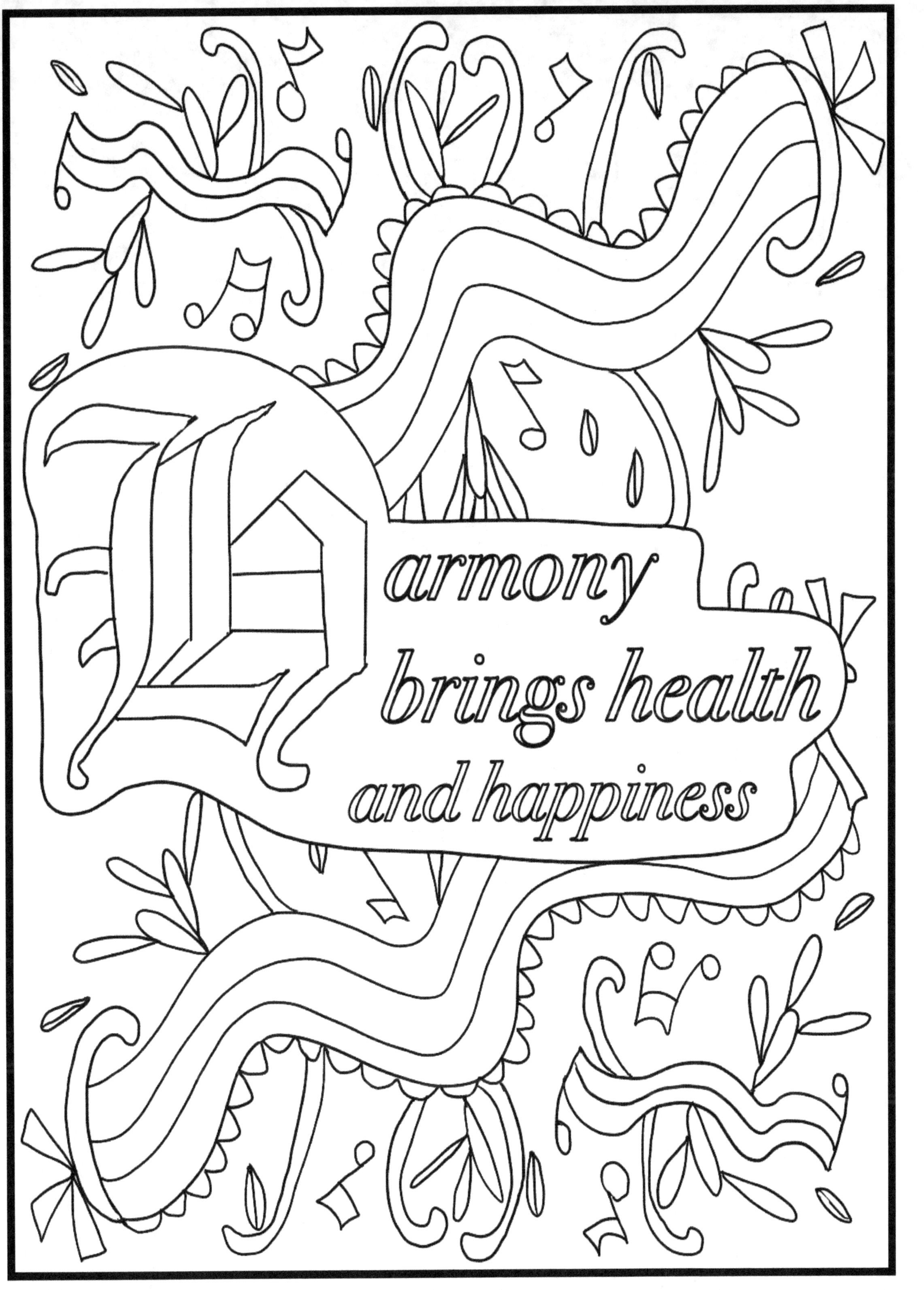
Harmony
brings health
and happiness

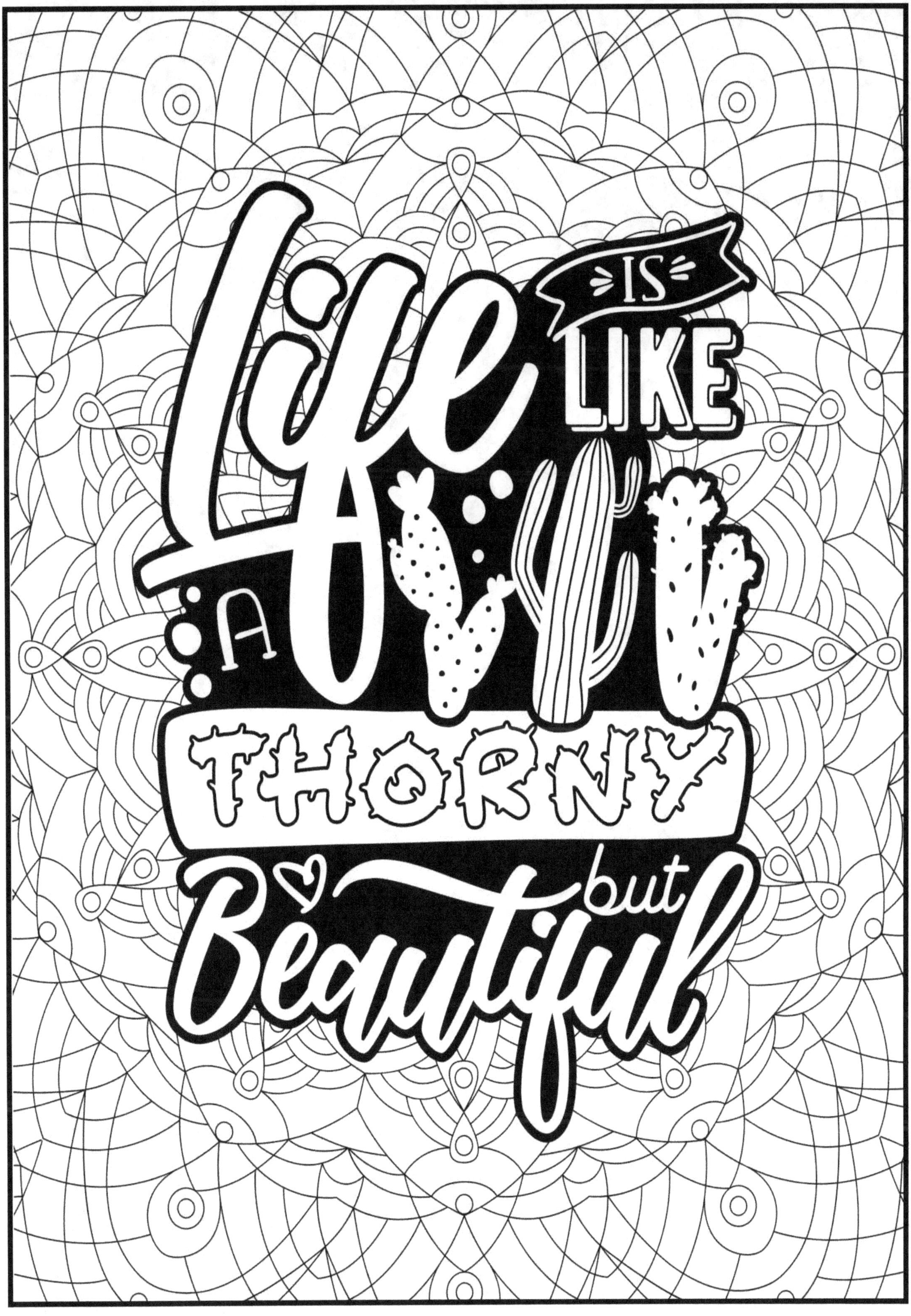
Life IS LIKE A THORNY but Beautiful

www.ingramcontent.com/pod-product-compliance
Lightning Source LLC
Chambersburg PA
CBHW081541220526
45467CB00010B/3279
9798692640420